C Instruments (Flute, Oboe and others)

CHRISTMAS CLASSICS

Easy instrumental solos or duets
for any combination of instruments

Selected by James Curnow

CURNOW®
MUSIC

Order Number: CMP 0964-04-400

Selected by James Curnow
Christmas Classics
Easy instrumental solos or duets for any combination of instruments
C Instruments

CD Accompaniment tracks created by James L. Hosay

CD number: 19-055-3 CMP
ISBN 978-90-431-2140-8

CHRISTMAS CLASSICS

Merry Christmas from Curnow Music Press!

What a joy it is to be able to use our God given talents, particularly during this joyous season, to celebrate the true meaning of Christmas. We are all so privileged to have such an incredible heritage of great Christmas music available to honor and praise the new born King.

This set of arrangements feature several of our excellent Curnow Music Press arrangers in new, fresh and dynamic settings of many of the traditional carols that you know and love. These arrangements are designed so that they can be used in two different ways, either as a solo or as a duet. Any combination of instruments can perform together. As long as each performer has the appropriate book for the key of their instrument, any combination of instruments will work.

An accompaniment book is available if you want to use a live accompanist. If an accompanist is not available, you can use the enclosed CD accompaniment. You will find creative and imaginative arrangements on the CD, which are useable in any performance setting. The CD can also be a useful tool for practicing when your accompanist cannot be there. At the beginning of the CD, you will find tuning notes so that you will be able to play in tune with the accompaniment. Each arrangement starts with a brief introduction to establish tempo.

I trust that you will enjoy this delightful collection of Christmas Classics, and that you will find many opportunities to use these materials to bring the joy of Christmas to everyone who listens.

Kindest regards,

James Curnow
President
Curnow Music Press, Inc.

Instrumentation Guide

C Instrument (CMP 0964-04-400)	- Piccolo, Flute, Oboe, or any Mallet Percussion instrument.
Bb Instrument (CMP 0965-04-400)	- Bb Clarinet, Bb Bass Clarinet, Bb Cornet, Bb Trumpet, Bb Flugel Horn, Bb Tenor Saxophone (play first part only), Bb Trombone T.C., Bb Euphonium/Baritone T.C., Bb Tuba T.C. (play first part only).
Eb Instrument (CMP 0966-04-400)	- Eb Alto Clarinet, Eb Alto Saxophone, Eb Baritone Saxophone (play first part only), Eb Tuba T.C. (play first part only).
F/Eb Instrument (CMP 0967-04-400)	- F/Eb Horn
Bass Clef Instrument (CMP 0968-04-400)	- Cello, Double Bass (play first part only), Bassoon, Trombone B.C., Euphonium/Baritone B.C., Tuba B.C. (play first part only).

Piano Accompaniment (CMP 0969-04-401)

Table of Contents

Tracks with second part and accompaniment (without first / solo part)

Tracks with accompaniment only

WESTMINSTER CAROL

Arr. **James Curnow** (ASCAP)

Moderately fast and stately (♩ = 104)

Solo

Duet

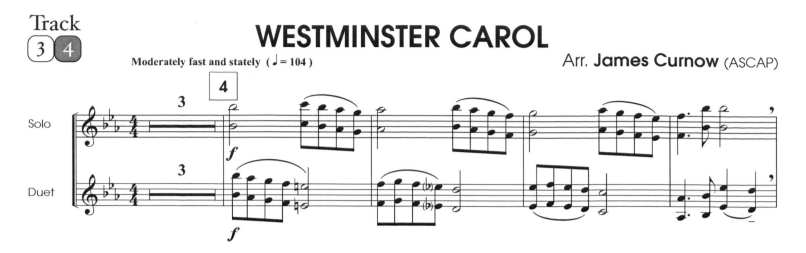

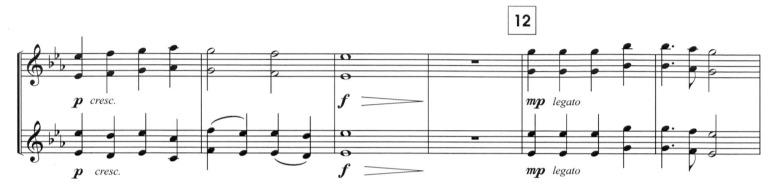

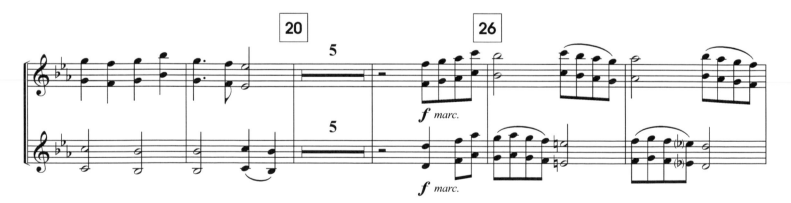

6

Copyright © 2004 by Curnow Music Press, Inc.

WESTMINSTER CAROL

O COME, O COME EMMANUEL

Arr. **Paul Curnow** (ASCAP)

Copyright © 2004 by **Curnow Music Press, Inc.**

O COME, O COME EMMANUEL

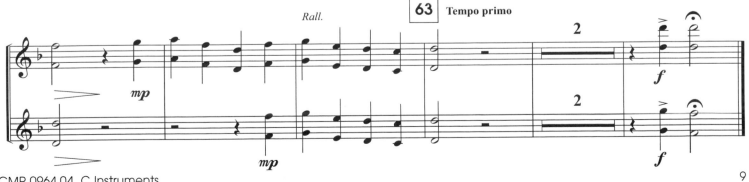

THE FIRST NOEL

Arr. **Timothy Johnson** (ASCAP)

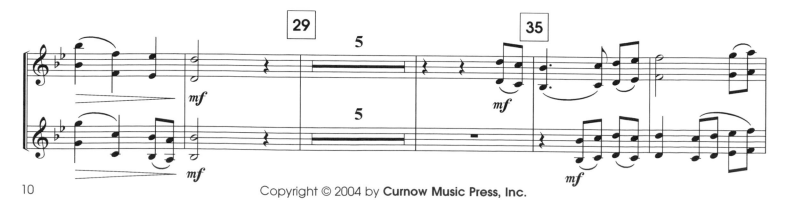

10

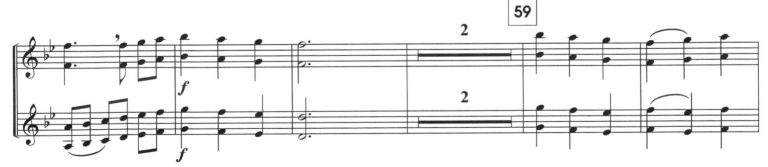

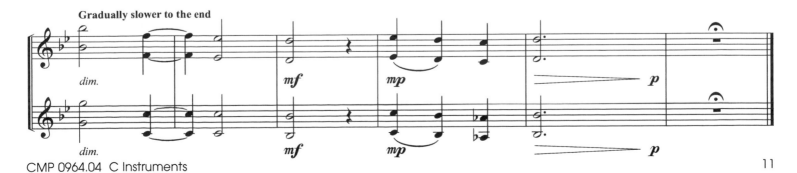

MARY HAD A BABY

Arr. **Stephen Bulla** (ASCAP)

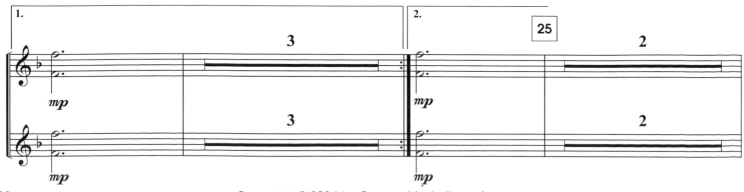

MARY HAD A BABY

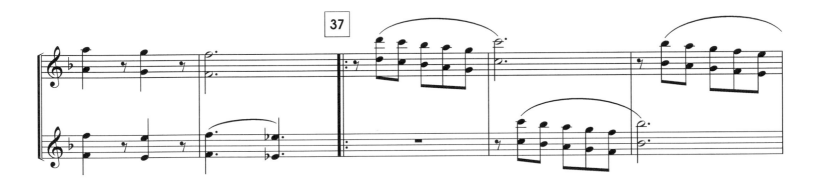

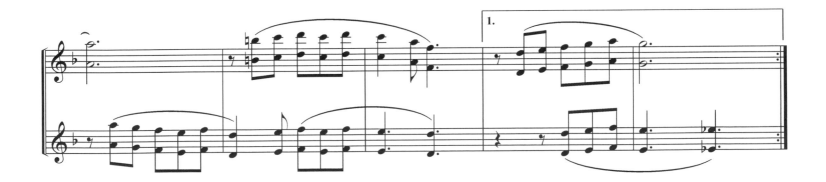

ANGELS FROM THE REALMS OF GLORY

Arr. Paul Curnow (ASCAP)

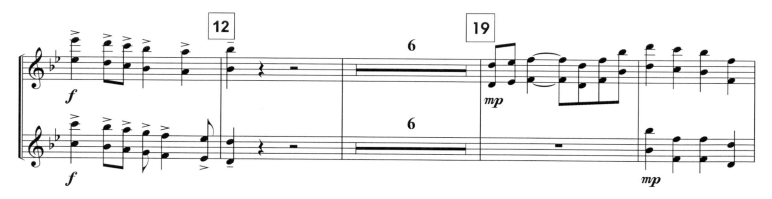

IN THE BLEAK MID-WINTER

Arr. **James Curnow** (ASCAP)

Moderately slow and sustained (♩ = 76)

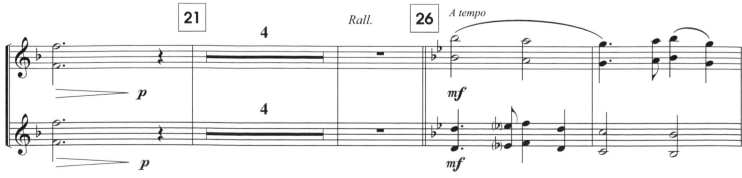

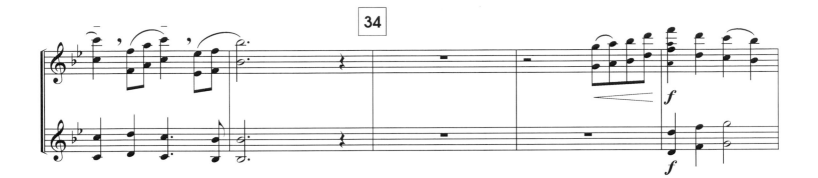

HE IS BORN

Arr. **Douglas Court** (ASCAP)

39

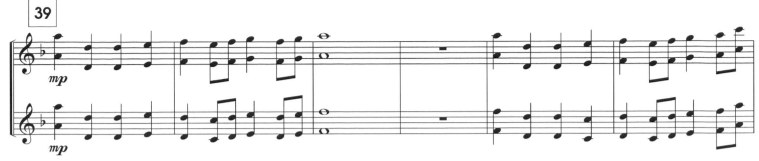

47

55 *If no 2nd, play cues*

63

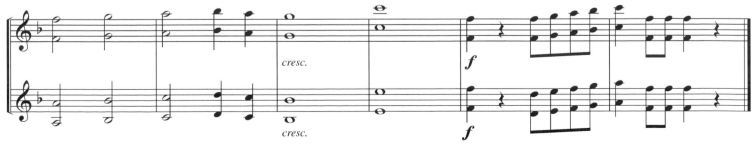

INFANT HOLY, INFANT LOWLY

Arr. **Paul Curnow** (ASCAP)

INFANT HOLY, INFANT LOWLY

GO TELL IT ON THE MOUNTAIN

Arr. **Stephen Bulla** (ASCAP)

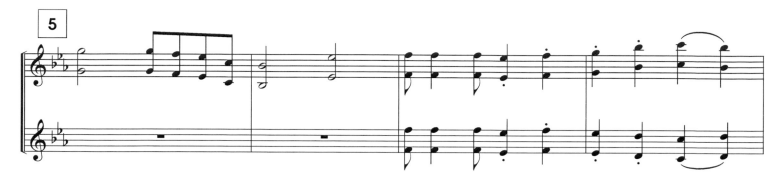

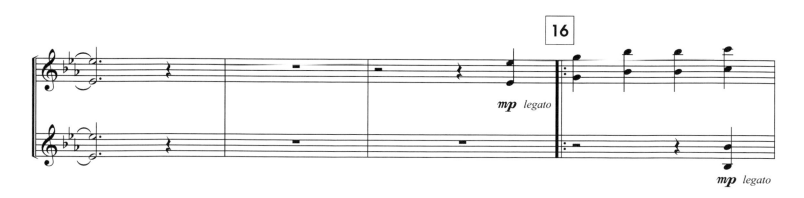

GO TELL IT ON THE MOUNTAIN

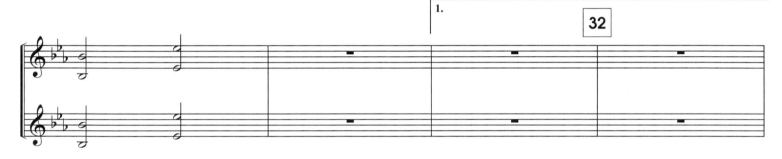

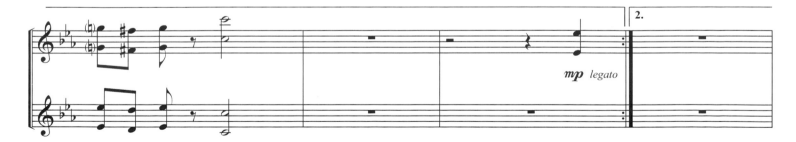

JOY TO THE WORLD

Arr. **Shawn E. Okpebholo** (ASCAP)

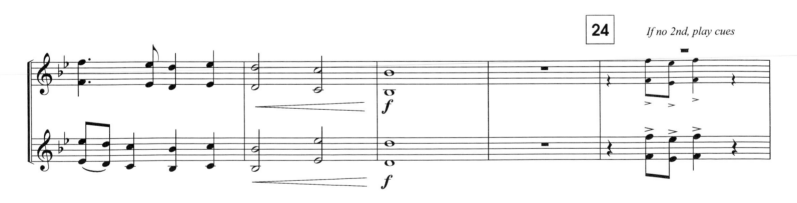

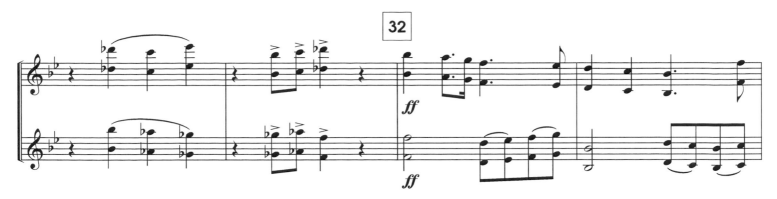

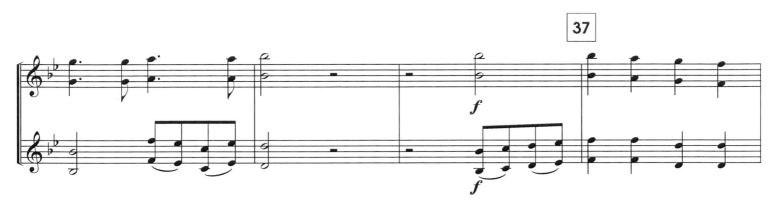

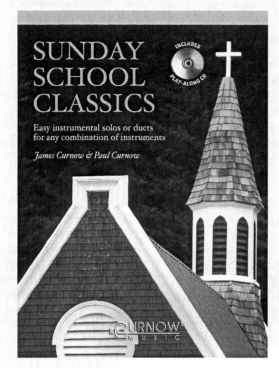

SUNDAY SCHOOL CLASSICS

These new arrangements of standard Sunday School songs provide the opportunity to play in many different styles, and to grow musically while performing in your church, or at other performance opportunities.

These arrangements are designed so that they can be used in two different ways, either as solos or as duets. Any combination of instruments can perform together. An accompaniment book is available if you want to use a live accompanist. If an accompanist is not available, you can use the enclosed CD accompaniment.

Available books:

C Instruments   (CMP 0658-02-400)
  (Piccolo, Flute, Oboe, or any Mallet Percussion instrument)

B♭ Instruments   (CMP 0659-02-400)
  (B♭ Clarinet, Bb Tenor Saxophone, Bb Trumpet, Euphonium T.C. and others)

E♭ Instruments   (CMP 0660-02-400)
  (E♭ Alto Saxophone, Eb Baritone Saxophone and others)

F Horn or E♭ Horn   (CMP 0661-02-400)

B.C. Instruments   (CMP 0662-02-400)
  (Bassoon, Trombone, Euphonium and others)

Piano Accompaniment   (CMP 0663-02-401)

CAMPFIRE CLASSICS

Campfire Classics is a collection of timeless campfire classic folk songs. They are delightfully arranged in fresh settings by two of the foremost arrangers in the instrumental field. These arrangements are designed to be used in two different ways, either as a solo or as a duet. Any combination of instruments can perform together. As long as each performer has the appropriate book for the key of their instrument, any combination of instruments will work.

The accompaniment CD (included in the solo book) provides two tracks for each tune. The first track includes the accompaniment with the duet part (for accompanying a soloist). The second track includes the accompaniment only (for accompanying a duet).

Contents:

Bingo / Kum Ba Yah / A Little R & R / The Itsy Bitsy Spider / She'll Be Comin' 'Round The Mountain / There's a Hole in my Bucket / Row, Row, Row Your Boat / Hush, Little Baby, Don't You Cry / Study War No More / Just Plant a Watermelon

Available books:

C Instrument	(Piccolo, Flute, Oboe, or any Mallet Percussion instrument)	(CMP 0934-04-400)
B♭ Instruments	(B♭ Clarinet, Bb Tenor Saxophone, Bb Trumpet, Euphonium T.C. and others)	(CMP 0935-04-400)
E♭ Instruments	(E♭ Alto Saxophone, Eb Baritone Saxophone and others)	(CMP 0936-04-400)
F Horn or E♭ Horn		(CMP 0937-04-400
B.C. Instruments	(Bassoon, Trombone, Euphonium and others)	(CMP 0938-04-400)
Piano Accompaniment		(CMP 0939-04-401)